Air Crashes

Elaine Landau

Franklin Watts
A Division of Grolier Publishing
New York • London • Hong Kong • Sydney
Danbury, Connecticut

For Areilla Garmizo

Note to readers: Definitions for words in **bold** can be found in the Glossary at the back of this book.

Picture Identification:
Cover: The *Hindenburg* explosion on May 6, 1937

Visit Franklin Watts on the Internet at:
http://publishing.grolier.com

Library of Congress Cataloging-in-Publication Data

Landau, Elaine
   Air Crashes / by Elaine Landau
       p.   cm.— (Watts Library)
   Includes bibliographical references and index.
   Summary: Explores such aircraft tragedies as the *Hindenburg*, TWA flight 800 and United flight 232, and looks at how we can improve airline safety.
   ISBN 0-531-20346-8 (lib. bdg.)   0-531-16416-0 (pbk.)
   1. Aircraft accidents—Juvenile literature. [1. Aircraft accidents.] I. Title. II. Series.
TL553.5.L274 1999
363.12'465—dc21   98-49174
                                            CIP
                                            AC

©1999 Elaine Landau
All rights reserved. Published simultaneously in Canada.
Printed in the United States of America.
1 2 3 4 5 6 7 8 9 10 R 08 07 06 05 04 03 02 01 00 99

Contents

A United Airlines jet takes off over the wreckage of Flight 232, carrying survivors and members of their family.

Safety in the Sky

Since early times humans have dreamed of flying effortlessly through the air. Modern air travel made this dream a reality, but the growing airline industry has had its share of problems. Mechanical failures, pilot error, and even terrorist acts have at times turned ordinary plane rides into tragic incidents.

While most travelers may lack the education to evaluate expert safety recommendations, simplified federal airline safety data became available on the Internet in 1997. The Federal Aviation Administration (FAA) posts information about airline safety, security violations, and accidents on its website. Searches may be conducted by aircraft type, weather conditions, or other related factors.

Yet is this information really useful to travelers? Many people believe that airline accidents occur too infrequently to be predictable. In mid-air collisions, the negligence of an overworked air-traffic controller may be more to blame than with a particular plane, pilot, or airline.

This book looks at several serious air mishaps. Each case examines the cause of these accidents and what can be done to prevent them from **recurring** in the future. The stories are sobering reminders that even with advanced knowledge and **technology,** completely risk-free air travel is still a dream of the future.

Chapter One

The Heavenly Hindenburg

Today they're called "blimps"—the huge, cigar-shaped, gas-filled balloons that often carry an advertiser's message across the sky. Years ago, blimps were known as airships, and were frequently used for air travel. In wartime, airships bombed enemy targets, patrolled coastal areas, and escorted naval ships through dangerous waters. **Civilian** airships with luxurious sleeping compartments and dining areas were used for regular passenger flights across the Atlantic Ocean.

The Hindenburg *glides near New York's Empire State Building.*

First-Class Travel

Traveling from Europe to the United States on the *Hindenburg* was always a luxurious experience. During the two-to-three-day trip, passengers enjoyed gourmet meals prepared by top chefs. Menus included lobster, prime cuts of meat, and wine. The *Hindenburg*'s twenty-five staterooms were beautifully decorated, and the ship's crew provided first-class service.

When airships reached the height of their popularity in the 1930s, the stately German-built airship the *Hindenburg* was among the largest and most elegant. The *Hindenburg* was as long as three football fields and weighed 240 tons.

Like many aircraft of its type, the *Hindenburg* was a rigid airship, built with a metal framework covered by an outer balloonlike skin. As with all airships, there was an element of risk in flying on the *Hindenburg*. Its outer skin, or envelope, was filled with hydrogen, an extremely **flammable** gas. If hydrogen comes in contact with a lighted match, it bursts into flames. However, the *Hindenburg*'s crew took extra precautions to ensure the safety of everyone on board. Passengers had to give up their matches or cigarette lighters when they stepped into the airship. "We Germans don't fool around with hydrogen," the *Hindenburg*'s chief **steward** had commented. A crew member even took a toy away from a young passenger because it gave off tiny sparks.

Captain Max Pruss, commander of the *Hindenburg*, was an experienced airship pilot. His fine reputation had been reported in a 1937 article in *Collier's* magazine, which also stated, "Only a stroke of war or an unfathomable act of God will ever mar this German [airship's] . . . passenger record."

The Unexpected Landing

Poor weather conditions delayed the *Hindenburg's* landing in the United States on May 6, 1937. Due to strong headwinds and thunderstorms along the coast of New Jersey, the airship did not receive clearance to land until 7:00 P.M. A number of people awaited the huge craft's landing at the Lakehurst, New Jersey, airfield. The group included a ground crew of ninety-

Spectators await the Hindenburg's landing.

A Great Feather

A radio announcer present at the scene of the explosion described the start of the airship's landing as follows: "Here it comes . . . and what a sight it is. . . . The ship's riding majestically toward us like some great feather."

two men, friends and relatives of passengers, news reporters covering the *Hindenburg*'s arrival, and an Associated Press (AP) photographer.

There are various reports about who was the first to see the fire as the airship arrived that evening. One spectator recalled noticing "a faint pink glow in the lower center of the ship . . . like some thick silvery fish with a rosy glow in its abdomen. It began small and pale, and spread redder and larger."

At the scene, an official from the U.S. Department of Commerce described the sight as a "puff-like flame . . . the size of a house door." Just seconds after witnesses noticed flames in the tail, that section of the airship exploded. Sixty seconds later, thirteen passengers, twenty-two *Hindenburg* crew members, and one of the ground crew lay dead amid the charred metal **wreckage** of the *Hindenburg*.

The exploding
airship begins
crashing to the
ground tail first.

The Survivors

Incredibly, some parts of the massive airship survived. Alice Hager, a science writer, was at the airfield that evening and remembered seeing "fire everywhere, rushing, sweeping its way through the pitiful crumpling wreckage. It was not possible that anything should be alive in that inferno," she noted. "Yet men leaped out."

Among the survivors was Joseph Spah, a thirty-two-year-old acrobat. His agility was tested when he crawled through one of the *Hindenburg*'s small windows and hung from a metal bar before leaping 50 feet (15 meters) to the ground. The escape of a fourteen-year-old *Hindenburg* cabin boy was also remarkable. He thought the burning debris would surely fall on him, when one of the water tanks suddenly burst, soaking him and extinguishing the flames around him so that he could get away.

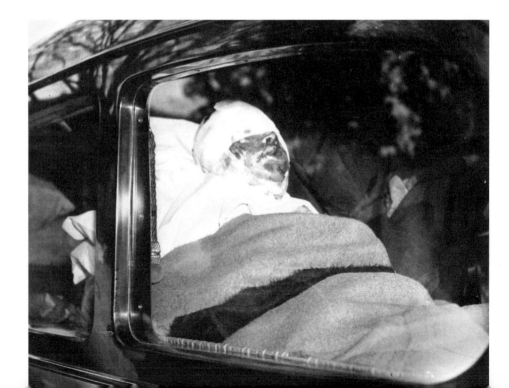

The Hindenburg's *captain, Max Pruss, is rushed to a local hospital.*

The Investigation Begins

Following the incident, there was a great deal of speculation about what had caused the explosion. After interviewing the survivors and examining the wreckage, the U.S. Bureau of Air Commerce announced that "a small amount of explosive mixture [hydrogen] in the upper part of the ship could have been ignited by . . . [an] electric phenomenon like a ball of lightning."

Many people were skeptical of the bureau's conclusions. They argued that since the *Hindenburg* didn't attempt to land until the thunderstorms had passed, lightning probably was

The Board of Inquiry investigates the charred remains of the Hindenburg.

13

not a factor. Instead, some individuals insisted that the *Hindenburg*'s destruction was an act of **sabotage** by enemies of the German government.

Could a small bomb have been planted on the airship before its takeoff in Germany? Undeniably, there had been threats against the *Hindenburg*, and some German submarines and airships had previously been destroyed or disabled by sabotage.

Bain's Theory

In 1997, sixty years after the *Hindenburg*'s destruction, a retired engineer named Addison Bain came up with another theory. Bain had worked for the National **Aeronautics** and Space Administration (NASA). After reviewing the survivors' testimony, Bain conducted tests on materials used in the airship's construction. He concluded that the explosion was due to neither sabotage nor an ignited hydrogen leak, the explosion was probably the result of the highly flammable substances used on the outer skin of the airship.

The variety of **synthetic fabrics** made today were not available in the 1930s. The cotton or linen used in airship construction was treated with a variety of chemicals to maintain and preserve the airship. The *Hindenburg* had been coated with **cellulose nitrate**, even though nitrate is used to make gunpowder. Aluminum powder, which serves as a fuel to launch a space shuttle's solid rocket boosters, was also used. When Bain tested materials coated in the same manner as the

Addison Bain traveled throughout the world buying original materials from the Hindenburg *to aid his research.*

Hindenburg's outerskin, they quickly burned. The retired engineer concluded, "I guess the moral of the story is—don't paint your airship with rocket fuel."

The End of an Era

Despite Bain's research, some experts still cling to their own theories about the *Hindenburg*'s destruction. However, one thing is certain—the *Hindenburg*'s crash marked the end of the era of luxury airship passenger travel. While the *Hindenburg* tragedy wasn't the first of its kind, aviation officials wanted it to be the last. Considered too dangerous to carry passengers, rigid airships were no longer built. They were eventually replaced by a wide variety of passenger airplanes.

United Airlines Flight 826

Chapter Two

The Christmas Crash

December 16, 1960

It was nearly Christmas, and airports across the United States were bustling with activity. People eagerly looked forward to wonderful winter getaways and holiday **reunion**s with loved ones. That's how it was for many of those heading from Columbus, Ohio, to New York City on December 16, 1960. Thirty-nine passengers would be flying on TWA's Super Constellation, sometimes affectionately called "Connie," a four-engine propeller plane developed in the 1940s.

The Connie's five-person flight crew was headed by Captain David A. Wollman, an experienced thirty-nine-year-old pilot. The passengers aboard Flight 266 included former newspaper reporter Richard Bitters, who worked at Ohio State University. Bitters wasn't supposed to have been on that flight. He had planned to fly to New York the day before, but his busy appointment schedule kept him in Columbus longer than expected. He felt fortunate to have booked a seat on the plane.

Technology of the 1940s

In 1947, the development of the Lockheed Constellation introduced nonstop coast-to-coast service. The Connie cruised at speeds of 270 miles (435 kilometers) per hour and **altitudes** of 22,000 feet (6,700 m). It used on-board **radar** to fly above and around bad weather.

Other passengers on the aircraft included an attorney, a young husband and wife with their two-week-old infant, some sales and public relations people, and several college students heading home for the holidays. For some unexplainable reason, Nancy Briggs, an attractive college girl, felt strangely uncomfortable as she awaited the flight. She told her boyfriend, who had taken her to the airport, that she felt they might never be together again. However, he thought her fears were groundless, and Nancy boarded the plane as scheduled.

A few people who were supposed to have been on Flight 266 had changed their plans at the last minute. One of these individuals was Walter D. Hunnicutt, who had moved to Ohio after retiring from National Dairy Products, a New York-based company. Although Hunnicutt usually returned to New York for the company's Christmas party each year, he had canceled his plane reservation after hearing it was cold and snowy there that day.

Everett L. McSavaney was another passenger whose flight plans changed abruptly. McSavaney, a law-enforcement officer, had been on his way to bring a New York prisoner back to Columbus. Just as he was about to board the plane, he received a phone call from headquarters instructing him to take another flight.

The DC-8

Less than fifteen minutes after TWA Flight 266 left the Columbus airport, a large United Airlines DC-8 jet took off

A Douglas DC-8

The New Jet Age

Introduced in the 1960s, the DC-8 (Douglas **Commercial** Number 8) provided passengers with twin aisles. Its high-technology **turbofan engines** allowed passengers to travel at air speeds of 550 miles (885 km) per hour at altitudes of 40,000 feet (12,200 m).

from Chicago's O'Hare International Airport, also bound for New York City. Aboard the DC-8 on Flight 826 was captain Robert H. Sawyer, an experienced, well-trained pilot, along with seventy-seven passengers and a crew of seven. Like the passengers on the Connie, some people were on board Flight 826 by sheer chance. One was eleven-year-old Steven Baltz of Willmette, Illinois. He was going to New York to spend Christmas with his grandparents. His mother and sister had flown into New York two days earlier. Steven was supposed to leave with his family, but since he had a bad cold and sore throat, it was decided that he should stay in bed for a few extra days before taking the trip.

Unidentified Object

While both the Connie and the DC-8 were headed for New York, they certainly weren't alone in the sky. That day, a New York Air Route Traffic Control Center reported more than fifty planes flying within 30 miles (48 km) of the city. The weather was not ideal for flying, as fog and sleet significantly reduced the pilots' visibility. Since many of the planes in the vicinity were heading for the same two airports, delays were anticipated. Some planes would have to maintain a **holding pattern** in the air until they could be cleared for landing.

United's Flight 826 was to land in New York's Idlewild Airport.

Ideally, the large DC-8 would reach New York's Idlewild Airport (renamed John F. Kennedy Airport in 1963), with only minor delays, while TWA's Constellation would land safely at LaGuardia, the other major New York City airport.

The first hint of trouble came from **air traffic control** at LaGuardia Airport when something unexplainable appeared on the radar screen. Immediately, the following message went out to TWA's Flight 266, "Unidentified target approaching . . . 6 miles." Soon afterward a similar urgent message was sent, "Unidentified object 3 miles . . . 2 o'clock.

Meanwhile, the United Airlines DC-8 was in contact with air traffic control at Idlewild Airport. After calling in its position, the aircraft was instructed to maintain altitude, and was given landing instructions. That was the DC-8's last official communication. Moments later, air-traffic controllers watched in horror as two blips on their radar screen merged and then disappeared. The unthinkable had occurred—United Airline's Flight 826 and TWA's Flight 266 had collided in midair. Apparently, both planes had been flying at the same altitude.

Dishes from the Sky

After exploding, parts of the Constellation fell on Miller Air Field, a helicopter airfield on Staten Island, an outlying New York City borough. The wreckage narrowly missed landing on two school buildings and a number of houses. A neighborhood

housewife said the impact sounded like "a thousand dishes coming from the sky." A local florist remembered that the plane came "tail-down, four propellers up and whirling helplessly . . ." Another witness added, "It went down in a terrible way . . . one wing gone, and it turned over very slowly."

Unfortunately, the downed DC-8 landed in a more densely populated area of the city. Parts of the jet hit an apartment building, while other pieces were scattered across the neighborhood's icy streets.

Pillar of Fire

The bulk of the flaming aircraft, hit a church located in the middle of the city and several other buildings, setting them on fire. Ironically, the church was named the Pillar of Fire Church.

The crash, which was the worst air disaster to occur up to that time, resulted in a **catastrophic** loss of life. A total of 127 people aboard both planes were killed instantly. Six others on the ground didn't have time to run for cover and save themselves. They included a city employee shoveling snow, along with two men selling Christmas trees.

A Christmas Miracle

In the midst of it all, witnesses also reported a seemingly miraculous occurrence. Steven Baltz, the eleven-year-old who had looked forward to Christmas with his grandparents, was alive. He had been thrown from the tail section of the jet into a snowbank. He was the only person on either plane to survive.

Passersby covered the boy with blankets and waited with him until an ambulance arrived. Later, with his parents at his side in the hospital, Steven had whispered, "The next time I fly I want to be my own pilot flying my own plane." But that was never to happen. Steven died a day later due to serious internal injuries.

Civil Aeronautics Board

What caused the tragic air crash that took so many lives and brought havoc to a peaceful neighborhood? Numerous charges and lawsuits were launched following the incident, but the results of the Civil Aeronautics Board's (CAB) investigation proved especially revealing. CAB blamed the DC-8's

Human error was the cause of this tragedy.

crew, whose pilot incorrectly reported the plane's position, and therefore, "proceeded beyond its clearance limits and the confines of the airspace allocated to the flight by Air Traffic Control." The aircraft had been traveling at a high speed, causing it to quickly pass through the **buffer** safety zone separating airport traffic. A trainee who had been working at

LaGuardia's air traffic control when the collision occurred, reported that although both LaGuardia and Idlewild were in contact with the planes, neither airport communicated with the other prior to the collision.

A Safer Sky?

As a result of the Christmas crash, airline safety measures were tightened. New speed regulations were set for planes approaching **terminals** and more air traffic controllers were required at busier airports. Improved airport communication systems were also installed so that air traffic controllers could safely switch planes from one airport to the next. In later years, three-dimensional radar systems were developed to further reduce the chances of midair crashes.

The surviving relatives sued the airlines, and a settlement of $29 million was reached, with United Airlines paying most of the damages. While the settlement was regarded as generous, no amount of money could ever return the lost loved ones to their families, or allow Steven Baltz to one day fly his own plane.

The body and tail section of Flight 232 is removed from an Iowa cornfield.

Chapter Three

United Airlines Flight 232

Sometimes a series of lucky coincidences can mean the difference between survival and disaster. This was especially true in July 1989, when the number-two engine suddenly exploded on a United Airlines DC-10 en route to Chicago from Denver.

Engine Two

The explosion was completely unexpected. Passengers heard a loud sound, felt a jolt, and then realized the plane was

This photo of Flight 232 was taken by a farmer seconds before the plane crashed.

The Big Four

After the stock market crashed in 1929, a new U.S. postmaster general realized the need for financially stronger airlines. As a result, the "Big Four" were created—United, American, Trans World Airlines, and Eastern. Seventy years later, three of the Big Four are still in existence.

tilting downward. Lori Michaelson, traveling with her husband and three children, described the occurrence, "I could see the stewardesses looked kind of panicky. That was understandable. One of them had been knocked to the floor." However, the captain's voice came over the speaker system moments later, assuring passengers that everything was under control. "We have lost the number two engine," he said. "We will be a little late arriving in Chicago."

Naturally, the captain wanted to keep the passengers calm. Engine number two was just one of three engines—any one of which could power the plane alone in an emergency. At first there seemed to be no real cause for panic. As it turned out, the loss of the number two engine would only be the beginning of United Airlines Flight 232's problems. Unfortunately, the explosion significantly damaged the plane's tail section causing a barrage of sharp metal fragments to rip through its **hydraulic** lines. Without a hydraulic system, the captain could not steer or control the plane.

Hydraulic Failure

Although the DC-10 had three separate hydraulic systems, the explosion destroyed all of them. The captain informed ground control that the plane was in "complete hydraulic failure," something that had never happened in the air before. Flight personnel were trained to handle the loss of one or two hydraulic systems, but there was no standard emergency procedure for a complete system failure. It looked as if the plane would simply crash, leaving no survivors.

A ground crew member inspects a plane's hydraulic system and landing gear.

"Brace! Brace! Brace!"

Once the pilot declared a state of emergency on board, ground control determined that he should try to land the plane at the Sioux City (Iowa) Airport. That meant the pilot and crew would have to do their best to maneuver the poorly functioning aircraft to its new destination. Luckily, fifty-eight-year-old captain Al Haynes was an exceptionally skilled pilot. He managed to steer the craft using brief thrusts of the engine. Another favorable factor was that United Airlines captain and pilot instructor Dennis Fitch happened to be on board. Assisting Captain Haynes and the first officers in the cockpit, Fitch got down on his knees and helped the crew manipulate the plane's **throttles**. Meanwhile, the Sioux City air tower alerted local law enforcement and medical emergency units to prepare for the crash.

The captain again spoke to the passengers, this time urging them to brace themselves for the crash. Just before landing he repeated the words, "Brace, Brace, Brace!" Four minutes later the DC-10 hit the ground in an Iowa cornfield, flipping over twice before finally coming to rest on its back. The plane had

Remains of the DC-10 are scattered across a cornfield.

broken into pieces. Only its nose, flight deck, and a portion of the passenger area were still recognizable.

Witnesses who saw the crash felt sure that no one could have survived, but they were wrong. Dr. David Greco, a leader of the Sioux City medical team, noted, "It wasn't real. We expected everyone to be dead and then . . . we saw all these people walking towards us from the corn. We thought, 'This is wonderful, a miracle.' " Incredibly, 185 of the 296 people aboard survived, and many of them were barely injured.

The Survivors

The Michaelsons were among the lucky ones. When the plane hit the ground, Lori Michaelson and her husband Mark unbuckled their seat belts, dropped to the floor, and led their two young sons out just before the plane burst into flames. However, once safely outside, they realized that their one-year-old daughter Sabrina was missing. Mark tried unsuccessfully to reenter the flaming wreckage to find her but, to the

Rescuers rush to aid survivors of the crash.

couple's relief, they found that another passenger had saved their baby.

Jerry Schemmel, who rescued Sabrina Michaelson, had also made it safely out of the plane, but didn't remain there very long. "I heard a baby crying," he explained, "and the next thing I remember, I'm back inside the plane. The baby was buried; she was in one of the overhead compartments of the plane with some debris on top of that. And I pulled that away and reached into the hole and pulled her out of there."

There was much to be thankful for. Yet all the survivors were keenly aware that fate had not been as kind to everyone on board. As Jerry Schemmel added, "[There was] a one-year-old boy sitting in the seat right in front of me on that plane and one moment he's looking over the seat playing peekaboo with me, and the next moment, he's dead."

Captain Haynes speaks at a press conference about his remarkable landing.

Life-Saving Factors

Having an exceptional pilot like Captain Haynes at the controls, along with Flight Instructor Dennis Fitch to assist him, has largely been credited with a landing that resulted in a remarkably high passenger-survival rate. One flight engineer said that Captain Haynes "belongs in the pilots' hall of fame."

Other factors were helpful too. Recent rain had dampened the cornfield, softening the ground and easing the impact of the crash. The

NTSB's Mission

The mission of the United States National Transportation Safety Board (NTSB) is to prevent future transportation accidents from occurring. When an accident or serious incident occurs, it is the NTSB's responsibility to investigate the crash, determine the probable cause, and make recommendations to prevent such accidents from ever occurring again in the future.

National Transportation Safety Board (NTSB) had also recently required that all planes have **fire-repellent** seat upholstery installed. These seats are believed to have saved many lives.

Federal Aviation Investigation

Following the Sioux City crash, a consumers group called the International Airlines Passengers' Association urged the Federal Aviation Administration (FAA) to check for possible design flaws in DC-10s. Only eight days after the Sioux City incident, a Korean Airlines DC-10 crashed in Tripoli, Libya. Later that same day, a Los Angeles DC-10 pilot reported hydraulic problems, although he managed to bring his plane down safely. The following day, an International Airlines DC-10 en route to Rio de Janeiro lost one of its landing wheels.

After an American Airlines DC-10 crashed outside of Chicago killing 273 people, the International Airline Passengers' Association won a court order that **grounded** all DC-10s until these planes could be inspected. Five weeks after the inspection, the planes were put back into service. The Sioux City

The FAA

On August 23, 1958, the United States Congress passed the federal act establishing the Federal Aviation Administration (FAA). The FAA regulates the training of all airline pilots, and is responsible for setting, reviewing, and enforcing Visual Flight Rules (VFR) and Instrumental Flight Rules (IFR).

crash again raised concern that McDonnell-Douglas, the plane's manufacturer, had incorrectly designed the aircraft by putting the three hydraulic lines together in the limited area of the plane's tail.

Today, many DC-10s are still in service. But many aeronautical experts believe that any problems in the DC-10s will vanish as newer and more sophisticated planes are introduced. They believe that computers will lessen pilot error, and advanced electronic technology will eliminate many mechanical weaknesses.

Another Chance

Many of the Sioux City survivors believe that the experience of surviving the crash has permanently changed their lives. Passenger Debbie McKelvey, who survived along with her two children, said, "Who can understand going through that, seeing bodies everywhere? You don't expect one 45-minute block of time to change your life totally, and it does. . . . People say, 'Oh, think you'll ever win the lottery? I say, 'I have.' " Her son Ryan McKelvey agrees, adding, "I feel I got another chance. I'm just making the most of it."

A DC-10 taking off from Chicago's O'Hare Airport lost one of its engines, killing all 273 passengers aboard.

Pieces of TWA's Flight 800 are lifted from the Atlantic Ocean.

Chapter Four

TWA Flight 800

On the warm, humid evening of July 17, 1996, sixteen members of the French Club at Pennsylvania's Montoursville High School, along with five chaperones, boarded a TWA 747 at New York's John F. Kennedy International Airport (JFK). They were heading for Paris, France—the trip of a lifetime for many of the students.

Others on TWA's Flight 800 were equally excited for their own special reasons. Andrew Krukar of Bridgewater,

Connecticut, was on his way to Paris with a sparkling diamond ring. He planned to propose to his girlfriend Julie Stuart. Andrew had shown the beautiful gemstone to some of his family, and now he took the ring with him on the Paris-bound plane, along with his hopes and dreams for a wonderful future.

Thirty-six-year-old Salvatore Mazzola was on the same plane, simply because a direct flight to his hometown of Palermo, Italy, hadn't been available that day. Having decided to catch a connecting flight in Paris, Mazzola could hardly wait to see his wife and his two small sons. Before leaving, he had called his wife to tell her how much he missed her and to inquire about his older son's shoe size. He wanted to bring the boy a new pair of shoes. But the child would never receive the gift.

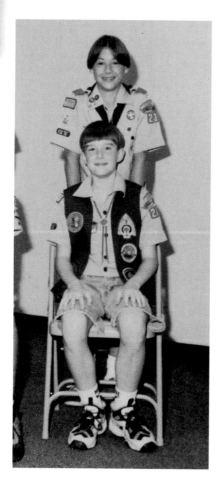

Victims of Flight 800 included young Thomas Weatherly and Joseph Scott (seated), of Stevenson, Alabama.

Also aboard the flight were Amy and Kyle Miller, both twenty-nine years old and on their way to Paris to celebrate their fifth wedding anniversary. Larkyn Dwyer, another TWA 800 passenger, was thrilled at the prospect of standing under the Eiffel Tower on her upcoming birthday. Ruth and Edwin Brookes, well-seasoned travelers from Edgartown, Massachusetts, were also on the flight that evening. The pair had already visited every continent in the world but Antarctica.

The lives and plans of all 230 TWA Flight 800 passengers were unexpectedly ended shortly after the plane took off. At an altitude of about 13,000 feet (3,962 m), the aircraft vanished from the air traffic controller's radar screen. The 747 had exploded in the air.

Disaster over the Atlantic

The explosion occurred over the Atlantic Ocean not far from the town of East Moriches on Long Island, New York. Rescue units, police, and firefighters quickly headed for the crash site along with local residents and fishermen. Cecilia Penney, who lived in the area, saw the explosion and remembered thinking, "Is this a nuclear war? It was like I was watching it on TV," she later commented.

Penney's husband, Randy, was among the volunteers who went out in a small six-boat rescue fleet. "The water was on

Remains of Flight 800 float along the Atlantic Ocean.

fire from the fuel," he recalled. Nevertheless, he and the others on his team managed to pull eighteen bodies from the sea. "We had to get them out of there quick because we didn't want them to sink," he explained. "I tried not to get a good look at them, at their faces. I didn't have time to think about what I was seeing—we were out there looking for survivors. And by about 3:00 A.M., it became apparent that there were none."

What Went Wrong?

Almost immediately, as might be expected, the victims' grief-stricken families, as well as the general public, demanded to know what had caused the fiery tragedy.

A pilot who had originally been scheduled to serve as first officer on the flight was switched at the last minute. He said, "That aircraft has had twenty-five years' experience without a

The Red Cross was called in to help grief-stricken families deal with their tragic loss.

catastrophic accident, and 747s just don't fall out of the air. There is nothing a crew member can do to make a plane blow up like that." Indeed, the Boeing 747 involved had a better-than-average safety record, and before TWA Flight 800, no 747 had ever crashed as a result of mechanical failure.

Some people speculated that the explosion was the work of terrorists. Before the plane left New York's JFK International Airport, it had come from an airport in Athens, Greece. The Athens airport was known for its careless security. Also, air traffic controllers had not received any pilot communication indicating a mechanical problem during the plane's last moments in the air. Another hint of terrorist activity was that some eyewitnesses thought they saw a surface-to-air missile go off in the plane's vicinity at the time of the explosion.

Flight 800's Formal Investigation

Following the crash, the most massive investigation in air-travel history was launched. Over the next seventeen months, experts carefully examined the **retrievable** wreckage looking for chemical **residue** that would point to a bomb.

They carefully examined all metal **components** at the crash site to see if parts of a timer or a bomb could be reconstructed.

In December 1997, the results of this exhaustive work were shared at open hearings of the NTSB in Baltimore, Maryland. There, scientists and engineers testified that the evidence conclusively proved that TWA Flight 800 could not have been destroyed by a bomb, a missile, or a meteorite.

The NTSB pieced the plane back together like a puzzle hoping to find the cause of the explosion.

Scientists concluded that the 747 exploded when fuel vapor in the plane's overheated center fuel tank was ignited by a spark. The researchers also added that the trail of flaming fuel produced by the explosion could have easily been mistaken for a missile by witnesses on the ground. The investigation further revealed that, for years, the aircraft industry had been aware that fuel vapor buildup in a jet's center fuel tank could create a serious safety risk.

The Missile Theory

In reaching their conclusions, investigators had evaluated information from eight radar sites around the northeastern United States, various radio transmissions, and the interior areas of the plane's wreckage. Michael Bott, a missile expert from the U.S. Navy base at China Lake, California, who had examined numerous downed warplanes, explained how the work proceeded. "Like every other investigator up there, I spent hours looking for every single piece that could point to [missile damage] . . . There's no large areas of missing structure on the aircraft that could contain all the damage from a warhead. Nor is there any place where a 'dud missile' could have hit the plane."

Metal specialists further confirmed these findings after weeks of examining the jet's center-section wreckage with a magnifying glass. James F. Wildey II, the senior metal expert at the NTSB described the flight remains as "some of the most-examined metal in the world," he noted. "Every inch, every quarter-inch of the center fuel tank was . . . [looked at] in great detail."

Safety for the Future

As a result of the investigation, government officials and aircraft manufacturers agreed to sharply reduce, or eventually eliminate, this potential air-travel hazard. The best available option may be to change the type of fuel presently used by commercial airlines to a fuel that would not change to vapor as easily. One such fuel, known as **JP-5**, is already used on U.S. Navy carriers. Air-safety experts think that JP-5 would reduce the risk of a center-tank explosion by about 95 percent. Airlines had previously resisted using the military fuel since it costs about two cents more per gallon, and the industry uses 67 million gallons (254 million liters) daily.

A groundcrew member refuels this military plane with JP-5.

49

Another safety precaution would be to add a spongelike foam inside commercial jet tanks. Since fuel tends to remain liquefied inside the foam, the foam might keep the fuel from turning into explosive vapor. The foam is already used in some military planes, and it could be adapted for civilian use.

Aside from enhancing air-travel safety, the NTSB hearings also offered a sense of closure to many of the victim's families. For nearly a year and a half, they hadn't known the full story behind their relatives' deaths. Judy Lychner Teller of Springfield, Illinois, who lost a sister-in-law and two nieces on TWA Flight 800, explained, "It's helped me bring together all the pieces of the puzzle . . . in a way that makes sense."

One year after the crash of TWA Flight 800, a memorial plaque was placed on East Moriches Beach, Long Island, in memory of the 230 victims.

Timeline of Aviation History

1896	Wilbur Wright designs and builds the first Wright flying machine
1902	The world's first powered, flying machine is built by Charles Taylor
1909	The Wright brothers sell the world's first military plane to the U.S. Army
1909	Louis Blériot makes the first flight across the English Channel
1914	Igor Sikorsky develops the first aircraft with an enclosed cockpit and flies the world's first four-engine aircraft
1915	World War I marks the development of the air combat era, featuring the French Spad 13, the British S.E. 5, the German Foker D.V. II
1918	The U.S. Post Office Air Mail Service begins operating between Washington, D.C., and New York
1919	Major airline activity begins
1926	The Air Commerce Act of 1926 establishes basic guidelines for commercial aviation
1927	Charles Lindbergh makes the world's first solo flight across the Atlantic Ocean, flying nonstop from New York to Paris
1927	Boeing Air Transport is founded by William Boeing
1928	Amelia Earhart becomes the first woman to fly across the Atlantic Ocean, accompanied by two companions
1929	The Big Four airlines are established—Eastern, Trans World Airlines (TWA), United, and American Airlines

1933	The DC-1 (Douglas Commercial No. 1), DC-2, and DC-3 are designed by Donald Douglas and Arthur Raymond
1937	The *Hindenburg* crashes and burns at an airfield in New Jersey, killing 36 people
1939–1945	World War II begins and ends as an air war
1953	A Canadian Pacific Comet Jet crashes, making it the first fatal crash of a commercial jet plane
1960	A United Airlines DC-8 jet and a TWA Super Constellation collide over New York, killing 134 passengers
1977	A KLM 747 and a Pan American 747 collide on the runway in Tenerife, Canary Islands, killing 582 people, making it the world's worst airline disaster
1985	A Japan Air Lines Boeing 747 crashes into Mt. Ogura, Japan, killing 520 people—the worst single-plane disaster in history
1988	A Pan Am Boeing 747 explodes and crashes in Lockerbie, Scotland, killing all 270 passengers
1989	A United Airlines DC-10 crashes while landing in a Sioux City cornfield, killing 111 passengers
1996	TWA Flight 800 explodes over the Atlantic Ocean, off the coast of Long Island, New York, killing all 230 passengers
1996	A Saudi Arabian Boeing 747 and cargo plane collide over New Delhi, India, killing 349 passengers—the world's worst midair collision
1998	Swissair MD-11 crashes into the Atlantic Ocean off the coast of Halifax, Nova Scotia, killing all 229 passengers

Glossary

aeronautics—the science and practice of designing, building, and fixing aircraft

air traffic control—a network of radio and radar navigation systems used to control flights of aircrafts from one airport to another

altitudes—the height of something above the ground

buffer—something that serves as a protective barrier

catastrophic—dreadful; disastrous

cellulose nitrate—a corrosive liquid acid used for making explosives

civilian—someone who is not a member of the armed forces

commercial—designed for a large market

component—part of a whole

fire-repellent—something that is made from material that will not burn easily

flammable—something that is easily set on fire and burns rapidly

grounded—to restrict to the ground

holding pattern—a course flown by an aircraft awaiting clearance to land

hydraulic—operated, moved, or affected by water

JP-5—a type of fuel used by the military that does not easily change to vapor

radar—a device used to find solid objects by reflecting radio waves off them and by receiving the reflected waves

recurring—to occur again

residue—remainder; what is left over after something has been destroyed or removed

retrievable—to rescue or salvage

reunion—a meeting of people who have been separated

sabotage—the deliberate damage or destruction of property, or an act that interferes with work or another activity

steward—a crew member who serves passengers on a ship or a plane

subsonic—of, relating to, or being a speed less than that of sound in air

synthetic fabric—material made with chemicals in factories

technology—the use of science and engineering to do practical things

terminal—a station at either end of a transportation line

throttle—a valve that controls the supply of fuel or steam going into an engine

turbofan engine—a type of aircraft engine in which a large fan pushes air into the hot exhaust at the rear of the engine, giving extra power

wreckage—the broken parts or pieces of something that has been destroyed

To Find
Out More

Books

Bailey, Donna. *Planes.* Austin, Texas. Steck-Vaughn Library, 1990.

Barrett, Norman A. *Flying Machines.* New York: Franklin Watts, 1994.

Coote, Roger. *Air Disasters.* New York: Thomson Learning, 1993.

Munro, Bob. *Aircraft.* Austin, Texas: Raintree Steck-Vaughn, 1994.

Oxlade. Chris. *Fantastic Transport Machines.* Danbury, CT: Franklin Watts, 1995.

Paulson, Tim. *How To Fly a 747.* New York: Norton, 1992.

Stacey, Thomas. *The Hindenburg.* San Diego: Lucent Books, 1990.

Tempko, Florence. *Planes & Other Flying Things.* Brookfield, CT: Millbrook Press, 1996.

Magazine Articles

"Brace! Brace! Brace!" *Time,* (July 31, 1989), p. 13.

"Terror on Flight 800" *Time,* (July 29, 1996), p. 34.

"Tragedy and Luck" *Newsweek,* (July 31, 1989), p. 19.

"What Really Downed the Hindenburg?" *Popular Science,* (November 1997), p. 74.

Organizations and Online Sites

The Aviation Home Page
http://www.avhome.com
Links users to airlines, airports, pictures of planes, books and magazines about planes, and flight simulation.

Boeing Company
http://www.boeing.com/
A great site for information on commercial airplanes, business airplanes, military airplanes, and missile/tactical weapons.

Earth Station 1: The *Hindenburg* Crash Radio Broadcast
http://www.mirrors.org.sg/earthstation/hindnbrg.html
This site features the entire live radio broadcast of the *Hindenburg* crash over Lakehurst, New Jersey, in 1937.

Federal Aviation Administration (FAA)
http://www.faa.gov
Homepage of the FAA posts information about airline safety, security violations, statistics, and other offices affiliated with FAA.

Florida Solar Energy Center
http://www.fsec.ucf.edu/bain.htm
Meet the researcher who discovered the cause of the *Hindenburg* disaster, Addison Bain. This site discusses his theory and his life as a NASA engineer.

A Note on Sources

In writing on disasters, various types of resources proved helpful. The books *Wide Body: The Triumphs of the 747* by Clive Irving; *The National Air and Space Museum* by C. D. B. Byran, and the *Dictionary of Aviation* by Ralph Nader and Wesley L. Smith, provided an in-depth look at the issue of passenger safety in the airline industry.

Sources for data and testimony on the actual disasters included *Eyewitness to Disaster* by Dan Perkes, *Disasters—Major American Catastrophes* by A. A. Hoehling, and *Man-Made Catastrophes* by Lee Davis.

Newspapers, magazines, and transcripts from which quotes and commentary were taken included, *Newsweek*, *Popular Science*, *Time Magazine*, The *New York Times*, and the CBS news show *48 Hours*. In addition, the Federal Aviation Administration (FAA) provided assistance in defining standards and specifications pertaining to airlines.

—*Elaine Landau*

Index

Numbers in *italics* indicate illustrations.

About the Author

Popular author Elaine Landau worked as a newspaper reporter and editor, and as a youth services librarian before becoming a full-time writer. She has written more than one hundred nonfiction books for young people. Included among her many books for Franklin Watts are the other Watts Library titles on disasters: *Fires, Maritime Disasters,* and *Space Disasters.* Ms. Landau, who has a bachelor's degree in English and journalism from New York University and a master's degree in library and information science from Pratt Institute, lives in Miami, Florida, with her husband and son.